REACTIONARY ESSAYS ON
POETRY AND IDEAS

REACTIONARY ESSAYS ON POETRY AND IDEAS

By

ALLEN TATE

Teaching the cause why all those flames that rise
From forms external can no longer last.
—THE OCEAN TO CYNTHIA.

Essay Index Reprint Series

BOOKS FOR LIBRARIES PRESS

FREEPORT, NEW YORK

LIBRARY OF CONGRESS CATALOG CARD NUMBER:
68-24856

PRINTED IN THE UNITED STATES OF AMERICA

To J. C. R.

FOR SUFFICIENT REASON

ACKNOWLEDGEMENTS

The essay on the late Hart Crane is made up of three papers, one written when *The Bridge* appeared in 1930, the two others after his death two years later. *Religion and the Old South* is a lengthened version of my contribution to *I'll Take My Stand* (Harper's, 1930), which is out of print. *Humanism and Naturalism* was published as *The Fallacy of Humanism* in Mr. C. Hartley Grattan's symposium *The Critique of Humanism* (Brewer and Warren, 1930). I am grateful to the editors of magazines in which parts of this book first appeared: *The New Republic, The Symposium, The Nation, The Virginia Quarterly Review, The Hound and Horn, The Criterion, Poetry: A Magazine of Verse,* and *The Southern Review.*

For critical reading of the manuscript I am indebted to Mr. Stark Young and to my colleagues, Professors A. T. Johnson, Samuel H. Monk, and W. T. Jones.

PREFACE

MODERN poets are having trouble with form, and must use "ideas" in a new fashion that seems wilfully obscure to all readers but the most devoted. The public waits to be convinced that the poets behave as they do because they cannot help it. That is one of the uses of criticism at the present time.

How have poets used ideas in the past? How are they using them today? How shall we explain the difference between the poet's situation in the past and his present situation? Or, if explanation is beyond us, as it probably is, what terms shall we call in merely to record the changes that have brought about the modern situation? It is, I think, our task to find out what the poets have done, not what they ought to have done, and to guess what it was possible for them to do in their times. But even the right guess would be a truism: what a poet wrote was alone possible for him to write. It is nevertheless a duty of the modern critic to notice the implication of the impossible, if only to warn the reader of modern verse, who is exasperated, that poets cannot write now like poets in 1579.

Poetry in some sense has a great deal to do with our experience. Historians exhibit its general features as evidence to support still more general theories of history and society. But modern literary critics are reversing the procedure of the historian. They are using social theories to prove something about poetry. It is a heresy that has, of course, reared its head before, yet never more formidably than now. We are trying to make a fine art respectable by showing that after all it is only a branch of politics: we are justifying poetry by "proving" that it is something else, just as, I believe, we have justified religion with the discovery that it is science.

Now to order our political interests is to practise one of the greater arts. Both politics and the arts must derive their power from a common center of energy. It is not certain that the old theory of art for art's sake is more absurd than its perfect analogy—politics for politics' sake, which as an abstraction becomes Economics that we pursue as truth-in-itself. It is agreed that our political confusion is alarming. It is not agreed that it will continue to be alarming until we are able to see our belief in the absolute of a scientific society as at least a phase, if not profoundly the cause, of our confusion. Both politics and poetry, having ceased to be arts, are cut off from their common center of energy. They try to nourish each other. It is a diminishing diet. The neo-communists are not likely to grow fatter on it than their capitalist brethren by giving it a new name. For a political poetry, or a poetical politics, of whatever denomination is a society of two members living on each other's washing. They devour each other in the end. It is the heresy of spiritual cannibalism.

This heresy is a legitimate field of modern criticism, but because it denies the traditional procedure of poets and is hence negative, it will concern the poet only in his faculty of critic, not in his job as craftsman. The poet's special question is: How shall the work be done? Why it was done and why the work is what it is, questions of first interest to readers of poetry, are of little interest to poets who are able to remain artists in a difficult age.

For poetry does not explain our experience. If we begin by thinking that it ought to "explain" the human predicament, we shall quickly see that it does not, and we shall end up thinking that therefore it has no meaning at all. That is what Mr. I. A. Richards' theory comes to at last, and it is the first assumption of criticism today. But poetry is at once more modest and, in the great poets, more profound. It is the art of apprehending and concentrating our experience in the mysterious limitations of form.

Philosophy even in the strict sense may be the material of poetry, but poets are not chiefly philosophers. A poet whose main passion is to get his doctrine—or his personality or his local color—into his poems is trying to justify a medium in which he lacks confidence. There is a division of purpose, and the arrogance of facile "solutions" that thinks it can get along without experience. The poet had better write his poetry first; examine it; then decide what he thinks. The poetry may not reveal all that he thinks; it will reveal all he thinks that is any good—for poetry. Poetry is one test of ideas; it is ideas tested by experience, by the act of direct apprehension.

There are all kinds of poetry readers. The innocent reader and the reader till lately called the moralist, who is now the social reader, are different from the critical reader, and they are both incurably intellectual. Their heads buzz with generalizations that they expect the poet to confirm —so that they will not have to notice the poetry. It is a service that the modern poet, no less amiable than his forbears, is not ready to perform: there is no large scheme of imaginative reference in which he has confidence. He must, in short, attach some irony to his use of "ideas," which tend to wither; he may look for a new growth but with the reservation that it too may be subject to the natural decay.

The innocent reader lives in the past; he likes to see in poetry, if not the conscious ideas, then the sensibility of a previous age. Our future sensibility the social reader, wise as he is, has no way of predicting, because he ignores the one source of that kind of prophecy—the present—grasped in terms, not of abstractions, but of experience; so he demands that poets shall set forth the ideas that he, in his facility, has decided that the future will live by. The poet— and it is he who is the critical reader—is aware of the present, any present, now or past or future. For by experiencing the past along with the present he makes present the past, and masters it; and he alone is at the center of the experience out of which the future must come. The social reader ought to remember that the specialist worries the major works of Spenser as a hungry dog his bone, but that the Divine Comedy has been at the center of our minds for six hundred years. The greater poets give us knowledge, not of the new programs, but of ourselves. A. T.

Southwestern
Memphis
February 16, 1936

CONTENTS

ESSAYS

FOUR AMERICAN POETS

I. EMILY DICKINSON

GREAT poetry needs no special features of difficulty to make it mysterious. When it has them, the reputation of the poet is likely to remain ambiguous. This is still true of Donne, and it is true of Emily Dickinson, whose verse appeared in an age unfavorable to the exercise of intelligence in poetry. Her poetry is not like any other poetry of her time; it is not like any of the innumerable kinds of verse written today. In still another respect it is far removed from us. It is a poetry of ideas, and it demands of the reader a point of view—not an opinion of the New Deal or of the League of Nations, but an ingrained philosophy that is fundamental, a kind of settled attitude that is almost extinct in this eclectic age. Yet it is not the sort of poetry of ideas which, like Pope's, requires a point of view only. It requires also, for the deepest understanding, which must go beneath the verbal excitement of the style, a highly developed sense of the specific quality of poetry—a quality that most persons accept as the accidental feature of something else that the poet thinks he has to say. This is one reason why Miss Dickinson's poetry has not been widely read.

There is another reason, and it is a part of the problem peculiar to a poetry that comes out of fundamental ideas. We lack a tradition of criticism. There were no points of critical reference passed on to us from a preceding generation. I am not upholding here the so-called dead-hand of tradition, but rather a rational insight into the meaning of the present in terms of some imaginable past implicit in our own lives: we need a body of ideas that can bear upon the course of the spirit and yet remain fixed as a rational instrument. We ignore the present, which is momently translated into the past, and derive our standards from imaginative constructions of the future. The hard contingency of fact invariably breaks these standards down, leaving us the intellectual chaos which is the sore distress of American criticism. Marxian criticism is, I believe, the latest disguise of this heresy.

Still another difficulty stands between us and Miss Dickinson. It is the failure of the scholars to feel more than biographical curiosity about her. We have scholarship, but that is no substitute for a critical tradition. Miss Dickinson's value to the research scholar, who likes historical difficulty for its own sake, is slight; she is too near to possess the remoteness of literature. Perhaps her appropriate setting would be the age of Cowley or of Donne. Yet in her own historical setting she is, nevertheless, remarkable and special.

Although the intellectual climate into which she was born, in 1830, had, as all times have, the features of a transition, the period was also a major crisis culminating in the war between the States. After that war, in New England as well as in the South, spiritual crises were definitely minor until the Great War.

Yet, a generation before the war of 1861–65, the transformation of New England had begun. When Samuel Slater in 1790 thwarted the British embargo on mill-machinery by committing to memory the whole design of a cotton spinner and bringing it to Massachusetts, he planted the seed of the "Western spirit." By 1825 its growth in the East was rank enough to begin choking out the ideas and habits of living that New England along with Virginia had kept in unconscious allegiance to Europe. To the casual observer, perhaps, the New England character of 1830 was largely an eighteenth-century character. But theocracy was on the decline, and industrialism was rising—as Emerson, in an unusually lucid moment put it, "Things are in the saddle." The energy that had built the meeting-house ran the factory.

Now the idea that moved the theocratic state is the most interesting historically of all American ideas. It was, of course, powerful in seventeenth-century England, but in America, where the long arm of Laud could not reach, it acquired an unchecked social and political influence. The important thing to remember about the puritan theocracy is that it permeated, as it could never have done in England, a whole society. It gave final, definite meaning to life, the life of pious and impious, of learned and vulgar alike. It gave—and this is its significance for Emily

5

Dickinson, and in only slightly lesser degree for Melville and Hawthorne—it gave an heroic proportion and a tragic mode to the experience of the individual. The history of the New England theocracy, from Apostle Eliot to Cotton Mather, is rich in gigantic intellects that broke down—or so it must appear to an outsider—in a kind of moral decadence and depravity. Socially we may not like the New England idea. Yet it had an immense, incalculable value for literature: it dramatized the human soul.

But by 1850 the great fortunes had been made (in the rum, slave, and milling industries), and New England became a museum. The whatnots groaned under the load of knick-knacks, the fine china dogs and cats, the pieces of Oriental jade, the chips off the leaning tower at Pisa. There were the rare books and the cosmopolitan learning. It was all equally displayed as the evidence of a superior culture. The Gilded Age had already begun. But culture, in the true sense, was disappearing. Where the old order, formidable as it was, had held all this personal experience, this eclectic excitement, in a comprehensible whole, the new order tended to flatten it out in a common experience that was not quite in common; it exalted more and more the personal and the unique in the interior sense. Where the old-fashioned puritans got together on a rigid doctrine, and could thus be individualists in manners, the nineteenth-century New Englander, lacking a genuine religious center, began to be a social conformist. The common idea of the Redemption, for example, was replaced by the conformist idea of respectability among

6

neighbors whose spiritual disorder, not very evident at the surface, was becoming acute. A great idea was breaking up, and society was moving towards external uniformity, which is usually the measure of the spiritual sterility inside.

At this juncture Emerson came upon the scene: the Lucifer of Concord, he had better be called hereafter, for he was the light-bearer who could see nothing but light, and was fearfully blind. He looked around and saw the uniformity of life, and called it the routine of tradition, the tyranny of the theological idea. The death of Priam put an end to the hope of Troy, but it was a slight feat of arms for the doughty Pyrrhus; Priam was an old gentleman and almost dead. So was theocracy; and Emerson killed it. In this way he accelerated a tendency that he disliked. It was a great intellectual mistake. By it Emerson unwittingly became the prophet of a piratical industrialism, a consequence of his own wordy individualism that he could not foresee. He hoisted himself on his own petard.

He discredited more than any other man the puritan drama of the soul. The age that followed, from 1865 on, expired in a genteel secularism, a mildly didactic order of feeling whose ornaments were Lowell, Longfellow, and Holmes. "After Emerson had done his work," says Mr. Robert Penn Warren, "any tragic possibilities in that culture were dissipated." Hawthorne alone in his time kept pure, in the primitive terms, the primitive vision; he brings the puritan tragedy to its climax. Man, measured by a great idea outside himself, is found wanting. But for Emerson man is greater than any idea and, being himself the Over-Soul, is innately perfect; there is no struggle because—I state the Emersonian doctrine, which is very slippery, in its extreme terms—because there is no possibility of error. There is no drama in human character because there is no tragic fault. It is not surprising, then, that after Emerson New England literature tastes like a drink of cambric tea. Its very center of vision has disappeared. There is Hawthorne looking back, there is Emerson looking not too clearly at anything ahead: Emily Dickinson, who has in her something of them both, comes in somewhere between.

With the exception of Poe there is no other American poet whose work so steadily emerges, under pressure of certain disintegrating obsessions, from the framework of moral character. There is none of whom it is truer to say that the poet *is* the poetry. Perhaps this explains the zeal of her admirers for her biography; it explains, in part at least, the gratuitous mystery that Mrs. Bianchi, a niece of the poet and her official biographer, has made of her life. The devoted controversy that Miss Josephine Pollitt and Miss Genevieve Taggard a few years ago started with their excellent books shows the extent to which the critics feel the intimate connection of her life and work. Admiration and affection are pleased to linger over the tokens of a great life; but the solution to the Dickinson enigma is peculiarly superior to fact.

The meaning of the identity—which we merely feel—of character and poetry would be exceedingly obscure, even if we could draw up a kind of Binet correlation between the two sets of "facts." Miss Dickinson was a recluse; but her poetry is rich with a profound and varied experience. Where did she get it? Now some of the biographers, nervous in the presence of this discrepancy, are eager to find her a love affair, and I think this search is due to a modern prejudice: we believe that no virgin can know enough to write poetry. We shall never learn where she got the rich quality of her mind. The moral image that we have of Miss Dickinson stands out in every poem; it is that of a dominating spinster whose very sweetness must have been formidable. Yet her poetry constantly moves within an absolute order of truths that overwhelmed her simply because to her they were unalterably fixed. It is dangerous to assume that her "life," which to the biographers means the thwarted love affair she is supposed to have had, gave to her poetry a decisive direction. It is even more dangerous to suppose that it made her a poet.

Poets are mysterious, but a poet when all is said is not much more mysterious than a banker. The critics remain spellbound by the technical license of her verse and by the puzzle of her personal life. Personality is a legitimate interest because it is an incurable interest, but legitimate as a personal interest only; it will never give up the key to any one's verse. Used to that end, the interest is false.

9

"It is apparent," writes Mr. Conrad Aiken, "that Miss Dickinson became a hermit by deliberate and conscious choice"—a sensible remark that we cannot repeat too often. If it were necessary to explain her seclusion with disappointment in love, there would remain the discrepancy between what the seclusion produced and the seclusion looked at as a cause. The effect, which is her poetry, would imply the whole complex of anterior fact, which was the social and religious structure of New England.

The problem to be kept in mind is thus the meaning of her "deliberate and conscious" decision to withdraw from life to her upstairs room. This simple fact is not very important. But that it must have been her sole way of acting out her part in the history of her culture, which made, with the variations of circumstance, a single demand upon all its representatives—this is of the greatest consequence. All pity for Miss Dickinson's "starved life" is misdirected. Her life was one of the richest and deepest ever lived on this continent.

When she went upstairs and closed the door, she mastered life by rejecting it. Others in their way had done it before; still others did it later. If we suppose—which is to suppose the improbable—that the love-affair precipitated the seclusion, it was only a pretext; she would have found another. Mastery of the world by rejecting the world was the doctrine, even if it was not always the practice, of Jonathan Edwards and Cotton Mather. It is the meaning of fate in Hawthorne: his people are fated to withdraw from the world and to be destroyed. And it is the exclusive theme of Henry James.

There is a moral emphasis that connects Hawthorne, James, and Miss Dickinson, and I think it is instructive. Between Hawthorne and James lies an epoch. The temptation to sin, in Hawthorne, is, in James, transformed into the temptation not to do the "decent thing." A whole world-scheme, a complete cosmic background, has shrunk to the dimensions of the individual conscience. This epoch between Hawthorne and James lies in Emerson. James found himself in the post-Emersonian world, and he could not, without violating the detachment proper to an artist, undo Emerson's work; he had that kind of intelligence which refuses to break its head against history. There was left to him only the value, the historic rôle, of rejection. He could merely escape from the physical presence of that world which, for convenience, we may call Emerson's world: he could only take his Americans to Europe upon the vain quest of something that they had lost at home. His characters, fleeing the wreckage of the puritan culture, preserved only their honor. Honor became a sort of forlorn hope struggling against the forces of "pure fact" that got loose in the middle of the century. Honor alone is a poor weapon against nature, being too personal, finical, and proud, and James achieved a victory only by refusing to engage the whole force of the enemy.

In Emily Dickinson the conflict takes place on a vaster field. Now the enemy to all those New Englanders was

Nature, and Miss Dickinson saw into the character of this enemy more deeply than any of the others. The general symbol of Nature, for her, is Death, and her weapon against Death is the entire powerful dumb-show of the puritan theology led by Redemption and Immortality. Morally speaking, the problem for James and Miss Dickinson is similar. But her advantages were greater than his. The advantages lay in the availability to her of the puritan ideas on the theological plane.

These ideas, in her poetry, are momently assailed by the disintegrating force of Nature (appearing as Death) which, while constantly breaking them down, constantly redefines and strengthens them. The values are purified by the triumphant withdrawal from Nature, by their power to recover from Nature. The poet attains to a mastery over experience by facing its utmost implications. There is the clash of powerful opposites, and in all great poetry—for Emily Dickinson is a great poet—it issues in a tension between abstraction and sensation in which the two elements may be, of course, distinguished logically, but not really. We are shown our roots in Nature by examining our differences with Nature; we are renewed by Nature without being delivered into her hands. When it is possible for a poet to do this for us with the greatest imaginative comprehension, a possibility that the poet cannot himself create, we have the perfect literary situation. Only a few times in the history of English poetry has this situation come about, notably, the period between about 1580 and the Restoration. There was a similar age in New England from which emerged two talents of the first order—Hawthorne and Emily Dickinson.

There is an epoch between James and Miss Dickinson. But between her and Hawthorne there exists only a difference of intellectual quality. She lacks almost radically the power to seize upon and understand abstractions for their own sake; she does not separate them from the sensuous illuminations that she is so marvellously adept at; like Donne, she *perceives abstraction* and *thinks sensation*. But Hawthorne was a master of ideas, within a limited range; this narrowness confined him to his own kind of life, his own society, and out of it grew his typical forms of experience, his steady, almost obsessed vision of man; it explains his depth and intensity. Yet he is always conscious of the abstract, doctrinal aspect of his mind, and when his vision of action and emotion is weak, his work becomes didactic. Now Miss Dickinson's poetry often runs into quasi-homiletic forms, but it is never didactic. Her very ignorance, her lack of formal intellectual training, exempted her from the risk that imperilled Hawthorne. She cannot reason at all. She can only *see*. It is impossible to imagine what she might have done with drama or fiction; for, not approaching the puritan temper and through it the puritan myth, through human action, she is able to grasp the terms of the myth directly and by a feat that amounts almost to anthropomorphism, to give them a luminous tension, a kind of drama, among themselves.

One of the perfect poems in English is *The Chariot,*

and it exemplifies better than anything else she wrote the special quality of her mind. I think it will illuminate the tendency of this discussion:

> Because I could not stop for death,
> He kindly stopped for me;
> The carriage held but just ourselves
> And immortality.
>
> We slowly drove, he knew no haste,
> And I had put away
> My labor, and my leisure too,
> For his civility.
>
> We passed the school where children played,
> Their lessons scarcely done;
> We passed the fields of gazing grain,
> We passed the setting sun.
>
> We paused before a house that seemed
> A swelling of the ground;
> The roof was scarcely visible,
> The cornice but a mound.
>
> Since then 'tis centuries; but each
> Feels shorter than the day
> I first surmised the horses' heads
> Were toward eternity.

If the word great means anything in poetry, this poem is one of the greatest in the English language; it is flawless to the last detail. The rhythm charges with movement the pattern of suspended action back of the poem. Every image is precise and, moreover, not merely beautiful, but inextricably fused with the central idea. Every image extends and intensifies every other. The third stanza especially shows Miss Dickinson's power to fuse, into a single order of perception, a heterogeneous series: the children, the grain, and the setting sun (time) have the same degree of credibility; the first subtly preparing for the last. The sharp *gazing* before *grain* instils into nature a kind of cold vitality of which the qualitative richness has infinite depth. The content of death in the poem eludes forever any explicit definition. He is a gentleman taking a lady out for a drive. But note the restraint that keeps the poet from carrying this so far that it is ludicrous and incredible; and note the subtly interfused erotic motive, which the idea of death has presented to every romantic poet, love being a symbol interchangeable with death. The terror of death is objectified through this figure of the genteel driver, who is made ironically to serve the end of Immortality. This is the heart of the poem: she has presented a typical Christian theme in all its final irresolution, without making any final statement about it. There is no solution to the problem; there can be only a statement of it in the full context of intellect and feeling. A construction of the human will, elaborated with all the abstracting powers of the mind, is put to the concrete test of experience: the idea of immortality is confronted with the fact of physical disintegration. We are not told what to think; we are told to look at the situation.

The framework of the poem is, in fact, the two abstractions, mortality and eternity, which are made to associate in perfect equality with the images: she sees the ideas, and thinks the perceptions. She did, of course, nothing of the sort; but we must use the logical distinctions, even to the extent of paradox, if we are to form any notion of this rare quality of mind. She could not in the proper sense think at all, and unless we prefer the feeble poetry of moral ideas that flourished in New England in the eighties, we must conclude that her intellectual deficiency contributed at least negatively to her great distinction. Miss Dickinson is probably the only Anglo-American poet of her century whose work exhibits the perfect literary situation—in which is possible the fusion of sensibility and thought. Unlike her contemporaries, she never succumbed to her ideas, to easy solutions, to her private desires.

Philosophers must deal with ideas, but the trouble with most nineteenth-century poets is too much philosophy; they are nearer to being philosophers than poets, without being in the true sense either. Tennyson is a perfect example of this; so is Arnold in his weak moments. There have been poets like Milton and Donne who were not spoiled for their true business by leaning on a rational system of ideas; that was because they understood the poetic use of their ideas. Tennyson tried to mix a little Huxley and a little Broad Church, without understanding either Broad Church or Huxley; the result was fatal, and what is worse, it was false. Miss Dickinson's ideas were deeply imbedded in her character, not taken from the latest tract. A conscious cultivation of ideas in poetry is always dangerous, and even Milton escaped ruin only by having an instinct for what in the deepest sense he understood. Even at that there is a remote quality in Milton's approach to his material, in his treatment of it; in the nineteenth century, in an imperfect literary situation where literature was confused with documentation, he might have been a pseudo-philosopher-poet. It is impossible to conceive Emily Dickinson and John Donne ever becoming that; they would not have written at all.

Neither the feeling nor the style of Miss Dickinson belongs to the seventeenth century; yet between her and Donne there are remarkable ties. Their religious ideas, their abstractions, are momently toppling from the rational plane to the level of perception. The ideas, in fact, are no longer the impersonal religious symbols created anew in the heat of emotion, that we find in poets like Herbert and Vaughan. They have become, for Donne, the terms of personality; they are mingled with the miscellany of sensation. In Miss Dickinson, as in Donne, we may detect a singularly morbid concern, not for religious truth, but for personal revelation. The modern word is self-exploitation. It is egoism grown irresponsible in religion, and decadent in morals. In religion it is blasphemy; in society it means usually that culture is not self-contained and sufficient, that the spiritual community is breaking up. This is, along with some other features that do not concern us here, the perfect literary situation.

II

Personal revelation of the kind that Donne and Miss Dickinson strove for, in the effort to understand their relation to the world, is a feature of all great poetry; it is probably the hidden motive for writing. It is the effort of the individual to live apart from a cultural tradition that no longer sustains him. But this culture, which I now wish to discuss a little, is indispensable: there is a great deal of shallow nonsense in modern criticism which holds that poetry—and this is a half-truth that is worse than false—is essentially revolutionary. It is only indirectly revolutionary: the intellectual and religious background of an age no longer contains the whole spirit, and the poet proceeds to examine that background in terms of immediate experience. But the background is absolutely necessary; otherwise all the arts, not only poetry, would have to rise in a vacuum. Poetry does not dispense with tradition; it probes the deficiencies of a tradition. But it must have a tradition to probe. It is too bad that Arnold did not explain his doctrine, that poetry is a criticism of life, from the viewpoint of its background: we should have been spared an era of academic misconception, in which criticism of life meant a diluted pragmatism, the criterion of which was respectability. The poet in the true sense "criticizes" his tradition, either as such, or indirectly by comparing it with something that is about to replace it; he does what the root-meaning of the verb implies—

he *discerns* its real elements and thus establishes its value, by putting it to the test of experience.

What is the nature of a poet's culture? Or, to put the question properly, what is the meaning of culture for poetry? All the great poets become the material of what we popularly call culture; we study them to acquire it. It is clear that Addison was more cultivated than Shakespeare; nevertheless Shakespeare is a finer source of culture than Addison. What is the meaning of this? Plainly it is that learning has never had anything to do with culture except instrumentally: the poet must be exactly literate enough to write down fully and precisely what he has to say, but no more. The source of a poet's true culture lies back of the paraphernalia of culture, and not all the strenuous activity of this enlightened age can create it.

A culture cannot be consciously created. It is an available source of ideas that are imbedded in a complete and homogeneous society. The poet finds himself balanced upon the moment when such a world is about to fall, when it threatens to run out into looser and less self-sufficient impulses. This world order is assimilated, in Miss Dickinson, as mediævalism was in Shakespeare, to the poetic vision; it is brought down from abstraction to personal sensibility.

Now in this connection it may be said that the prior conditions for great poetry, given a great talent, are just two: the thoroughness of the poet's discipline in an objective system of truth, and his lack of consciousness of such a discipline. For this discipline is a number of fundamental ideas the origin of which the poet does not know; they give form and stability to his fresh perceptions of the world; and he cannot shake them off. This is his culture, and like Tennyson's God it is nearer than hands and feet. With reasonable certainty we unearth the elements of Shakespeare's culture, and yet it is equally certain—so innocent was he of his own resources—that he would not know what our discussion is about. He appeared at the collapse of the mediæval system as a rigid pattern of life, but that pattern remained in Shakespeare what Shelley called a "fixed point of reference" for his sensibility. Miss Dickinson, as we have seen, was born into the equilibrium of an old and a new order. Puritanism could not be to her what it had been to the generation of Cotton Mather—a body of absolute truths; it was an unconscious discipline timed to the pulse of her life.

The perfect literary situation—that is what it is: it produces, because it is rare, a special and perhaps the most distinguished kind of poet. I am not trying to invent a new critical category. Such poets are never very much alike on the surface; they show us all the varieties of poetic feeling; and like other poets they resist all classification but that of temporary convenience. But, I believe, Miss Dickinson and John Donne would have this in common: their sense of the natural world is not blunted by a too rigid system of ideas; yet the ideas, the abstractions, their education or their intellectual heritage, are not so weak as to let their immersion in nature, or their purely personal quality, get out of control. The two poles of the mind are not separately visible; we infer them from the lucid tension that may be most readily illustrated by polar activity. There is no thought as such at all; nor is there feeling; there is that unique focus of experience which is at once neither and both.

Like Miss Dickinson, Shakespeare has no opinions whatever; his peculiar merit too is deeply involved in his failure to think about anything; his meaning is not in the content of his expression; it is in the tension of the dramatic relations of his characters. This kind of poetry is at the opposite of intellectualism. (Miss Dickinson is obscure and difficult, but that is not intellectualism.) To T. W. Higginson, the editor of *The Atlantic Monthly,* who tried to advise her, she wrote that she had no education. In any sense that Higginson could understand, it was quite true. His kind of education was the conscious cultivation of abstractions. She did not reason about the world she saw; she merely saw it. The "ideas" implicit in the world within her rose up, concentrated in her slightest perception.

That kind of world at present has for us something of the fascination of a buried city. There is none like it. When such worlds exist, when such cultures flourish, they support not only the poet but all members of society. For, from these, the poet differs only in his gift for exhibiting the structure, the internal lineaments, of his culture by threatening to tear them apart: a process that concentrates the symbolic emotions of society while it seems to attack them. The poet may hate his age; he may be an outcast like Villon; but this world is always there as the background to what he has to say. It is the lens through which he brings nature to focus and control—the clarifying medium that concentrates his personal feeling. It is ready-made; he cannot make it; with it, his poetry has a spontaneity and a certainty of direction that, without it, it would lack. No poet could have invented the elements of *The Chariot;* only a great poet could have used them so perfectly. Miss Dickinson was a deep mind writing from a deep culture, and when she came to poetry, she came infallibly.

Infallibly, at her best; for no poet has ever been perfect, nor is Emily Dickinson. Her unsurpassed precision of statement is due to the directness with which the abstract framework of her thought acts upon its unorganized material. The two elements of her style, considered as point of view, are immortality, or the idea of permanence, and the physical process of death or decay. Her diction has two corresponding features: words of Latin or Greek origin and, sharply opposed to these, the concrete Saxon element. It is this verbal conflict that gives to her verse its high tension; it is not a device deliberately seized upon, but a feeling for language that senses out the two fundamental components of English and their metaphysical relation: the Latin for ideas and the Saxon for perceptions—the peculiar virtue of English as a poetic tongue. Only the great poets know how to use this advantage of our language.

Like all poets, Miss Dickinson often writes out of habit;

the style that emerged from some deep exploration of an idea is carried on as verbal habit when she has nothing to say. She indulges herself:

> There's something quieter than sleep
> Within this inner room!
> It wears a sprig upon its breast,
> And will not tell its name.
>
> Some touch it and some kiss it,
> Some chafe its idle hand;
> It has a simple gravity
> I do not understand!
>
> While simple hearted neighbors
> Chat of the 'early dead,'
> We, prone to periphrasis,
> Remark that birds have fled!

It is only a pert remark; at best a superior kind of punning—one of the worst specimens of her occasional interest in herself.

But she never had the slightest interest in the public. Were four poems or five published in her lifetime? She never felt the temptation to round off a poem for public exhibition. Higginson's kindly offer to make her verse "correct" was an invitation to throw her work into the public ring—the ring of Lowell and Longfellow. He could not see that he was tampering with one of the rarest literary integrities of all time. Here was a poet who had no use for the supports of authorship—flattery and fame; she never needed money.

She had all the elements of a culture that has broken up, a culture that on the religious side takes its place in the museum of spiritual antiquities. Puritanism, as a unified version of the world, is dead; only a remnant of it in trade may be said to survive. In the history of puritanism she comes between Hawthorne and Emerson. She has Hawthorne's matter, which a too irresponsible personality tends to dilute into a form like Emerson's; she is often betrayed by words. But she is not the poet of personal sentiment; she has more to say than she can put down in any one poem. Like Hardy and Whitman she must be read entire; like Shakespeare she never gives up her meaning in a single line.

She is therefore a perfect subject for the kind of criticism which is chiefly concerned with general ideas. She exhibits one of the permanent relations between personality and objective truth, and she deserves the special attention of our time, which lacks that kind of truth.

She has Hawthorne's intellectual toughness, a hard, definite sense of the physical world. The highest flights to God, the most extravagant metaphors of the strange and the remote, come back to a point of casuistry, to a moral dilemma of the experienced world. There is, in spite of the homiletic vein of utterance, no abstract speculation, nor is there a message to society; she speaks wholly to the individual experience. She offers to the unimaginative no riot of vicarious sensation; she has no useful maxims for men of action. Up to this point her resemblance to Emerson is slight: poetry is a sufficient form of utterance, and her devotion to it is pure. But in **Emily Dickinson** the puritan world is no longer self-contained; it is no longer complete; her sensibility exceeds its dimensions. She has trimmed down its supernatural proportions; it has become a morality; instead of the tragedy of the spirit there is a commentary upon it. Her poetry is a magnificent personal confession, blasphemous and, in its self-revelation, its implacable honesty, almost obscene. It comes out of an intellectual life towards which it feels no moral responsibility. Mather would have burnt her for a witch.

II. HART CRANE

THE career of Hart Crane will be written by future critics as a chapter in the neo-symbolist movement. An historical view of his poetry at this time would be misleading and incomplete. Like most poets of his age in America, Crane discovered Rimbaud through Eliot and the Imagists; it is certain that long before he had done any of his best work he had come to believe himself the spiritual heir of the French poet. While it is true that he mastered the symbolist use of fused metaphor, it is also true that this is a feature of all poetic language. Whether Crane's style is symbolistic, or should, in many instances, like the first six or seven stanzas of *The River,* be called Elizabethan, is a question that need not concern us now.

Between *The Bridge* and *Une Saison d'Enfer* there is little essential affinity. Rimbaud achieved "disorder" out of implicit order, after a deliberate cultivation of "derangement," but in our time the disintegration of our intellectual systems is accomplished. With Crane the disorder is original and fundamental. That is the special quality of his mind that belongs peculiarly to our own time. His æsthetic problem, however, was more general; it was the historic problem of romanticism.

Harold Hart Crane, one of the great masters of the romantic movement, was born in Garrettsville, Ohio, on

July 21, 1899. His birthplace is a small town near Cleveland, in the old Western Reserve, a region which, as distinguished from the lower portions of the state, where people from the Southern up-country settled, was populated largely by New England stock. He seems to have known little of his ancestry, but he frequently said that his maternal forbears had given Hartford, Connecticut, its name, and that they went "back to Stratford-on-Avon" —a fiction surely, but one that gave him distinct pleasure. His formal education was slight. After the third year at high school, when he was fifteen, it ended, and he worked in his father's candy factory in Cleveland, where the family had removed in his childhood. He repeatedly told me that money had been set aside for his education at college, but that it had been used for other purposes. With the instinct of genius he read the great poets, but he never acquired an objective mastery of any literature, or even of the history of his country—a defect of considerable interest in a poet whose most ambitious work is an American epic.

In any ordinary sense Crane was not an educated man; in many respects he was an ignorant man. There is already a Crane legend, like the Poe legend—it should be fostered because it will help to make his poetry generally known—and the scholars will decide it was a pity that so great a talent lacked early advantages. It is probable that he was incapable of the formal discipline of a classical education, and probable, too, that the eclectic education of his time would have scattered and killed his talent.

His poetry not only has defects of the surface, it has a defect of vision; but its great and peculiar value cannot be separated from its limitations. Its qualities are bound up with a special focus of the intellect and sensibility, and it would be foolish to wish that his mind had been better trained or differently organized.

The story of his suicide is well known. The information that I have seems authentic, but it is incomplete and subject to excessive interpretation. Toward the end of April, 1932, he embarked on the S.S. *Orizaba* bound from Vera Cruz to New York. On the night of April 26 he got into a brawl with some sailors; he was severely beaten and robbed. At noon the next day, the ship being in the Caribbean a few hours out of Havana, he rushed from his stateroom clad in pajamas and overcoat, walked through the smoking-room out onto the deck, and then the length of the ship to the stern. There without hesitation he made a perfect dive into the sea. It is said that a life-preserver was thrown to him; he either did not see it or did not want it. By the time the ship had turned back he had disappeared. Whether he forced himself down—for a moment he was seen swimming—or was seized by a shark, as the captain believed, cannot be known. After a search of thirty-five minutes his body was not found, and the *Orizaba* put back into her course.

In the summer of 1930 he had written to me that he feared his most ambitious work, *The Bridge*, was not quite perfectly "realized," that probably his soundest work was in the shorter pieces of *White Buildings*, but that his mind, being once committed to the larger undertaking, could never return to the lyrical and more limited form. He had an extraordinary insight into the foundations of his work, and I think this judgment of it will not be refuted.

From 1922 to 1928—after that year I saw him and heard from him irregularly until his death—I could observe the development of his style from poem to poem; and his letters—written always in a pure and lucid prose —provide a valuable commentary on his career. This is not the place to bring all this material together for judgment. As I look back upon his work and its relation to the life he lived, a general statement about it comes to my mind that may throw some light on the dissatisfaction that he felt with his career. It will be a judgment upon the life and works of a man whom I knew for ten years as a friend.

Suicide was the sole act of will left to him short of a profound alteration of his character. I think the evidence of this is the locked-in sensibility, the insulated egoism, of his poetry—a subject that I shall return to. The background of his death was dramatically perfect: a large portion of his finest imagery was of the sea, chiefly the Caribbean:

> O minstrel galleons of Carib fire,
> Bequeath us to no earthly shore until
> Is answered in the vortex of our grave
> The seal's wide spindrift gaze towards paradise.

His verse is full of splendid images of this order, a rich

symbolism for an implicit pantheism that, whatever may be its intrinsic merit, he had the courage to vindicate with death in the end.

His pantheism was not passive and contemplative; it rose out of the collision between his own locked-in sensibility and the ordinary forms of experience. Every poem is a thrust of that sensibility into the world: his defect lay in his inability to face out the moral criticism implied in the failure to impose his will upon experience.

The Bridge is presumably an epic. How early he had conceived the idea of the poem and the leading symbolism, it is difficult to know; certainly as early as February, 1923. Up to that time, with the exception of *For the Marriage of Faustus and Helen* (1922), he had written only short poems, but most of them, *Praise for an Urn, Black Tambourine, Paraphrase,* and *Emblems of Conduct,* are among his finest work. It is a mistake then to suppose that all of *White Buildings* is early experimental writing; a large portion of that volume, and perhaps the least successful part of it, is made up of poems written after *The Bridge* was begun. *Praise for an Urn* was written in the spring of 1922—one of the finest elegies by an American poet—and although his later development gave us a poetry that the period would be much the less rich for not having, he never again had such perfect mastery of his subject—because he never again knew precisely what his subject was.

Readers familiar with *For the Marriage of Faustus and Helen* admire it by passages, but the form of the poem, in its framework of symbol, is an abstraction empty of any knowable experience. It is a conventional revival of the kind of diction that a young poet picks up in his first reading. Crane, I believe, felt that this was so; and he became so dissatisfied, not only with the style of the poem, which is heavily influenced by Eliot and Laforgue, but with the "literary" character of the symbolism, that he set about the greater task of writing *The Bridge*. He had looked upon his *Faustus and Helen* as an answer to the cultural pessimism of the school of Eliot, and *The Bridge* was to be an even more complete answer.

There was a fundamental mistake in Crane's diagnosis of Eliot's problem. Eliot's "pessimism" grows out of an awareness of the decay of the individual consciousness and its fixed relations to the world; but Crane thought that it was due to something like pure "orneryness," an unwillingness "to share with us the breath released," the breath being a new kind of freedom that he identified emotionally with the age of the machine. This vagueness of purpose, in spite of the apparently concrete character of the Brooklyn Bridge, which became the symbol of his epic, he never succeeded in correcting. The "bridge" stands for no well-defined experience; it differs from the Helen and Faust symbols only in its unliterary origin. I think Crane was deceived by this difference, and by the fact that Brooklyn Bridge is "modern" and a fine piece of "mechanics." His more ambitious later project permitted him no greater degree of formal structure than the more literary symbolism of his youth.

The fifteen parts of *The Bridge* taken as one poem suffer from the lack of a coherent structure, whether symbolic or narrative: the coherence of the work consists in the personal quality of the writing—in mood, feeling, and tone. In the best passages Crane has perfect mastery over the quality of his style; but it lacks an objective pattern of ideas elaborate enough to carry it through an epic or heroic work. The single symbolic image, in which the whole poem centers, is at one moment the actual Brooklyn Bridge; at another, it is any bridge or "connection"; at still another, it is a philosophical pun and becomes the basis of a series of analogies.

In *Cape Hatteras,* the aëroplane and Walt Whitman are analogous "bridges" to some transcendental truth. Because the idea is variously metaphor, symbol, and analogy, it tends to make the poem static. The poet takes it up, only to be forced to put it down again *when the poetic image of the moment is exhausted.* The idea does not, in short, fill the poet's mind; it is the starting point for a series of short flights, or inventions connected only in analogy—which explains the merely personal passages, which are obscure, and the lapses into sentimentality. For poetic sentimentality is emotion undisciplined by the structure of events or ideas of which it is ostensibly a part. The idea is not objective and articulate in itself; it lags after the poet's vision; it appears and disappears; and in the intervals Crane improvises, often beautifully, as in the flight of the aëroplane, sometimes badly, as in the passage on Whitman in the same poem.

In the great epic and philosophical works of our tradition, notably the *Divine Comedy,* the intellectual groundwork is not only simple philosophically; we not only know that the subject is personal salvation, just as we know that Crane's is the greatness of America: we are given also the complete articulation of the idea down to the slightest detail, and we are given it objectively apart from anything that the poet is going to say about it. When the poet extends his perception, there is a further extension of the groundwork ready to meet it and discipline it, and to compel the sensibility of the poet to stick to the subject. It is a game of chess; neither side can move without consulting the other. Crane's difficulty is that of modern poets generally: they play the game with half of the men, the men of sensibility, and because sensibility can make any move, the significance of all moves is obscure.

If we subtract from Crane's idea its periphery of sensation, we have left only the dead abstraction, the Greatness of America, which is capable of elucidation neither on the logical plane nor in terms of a generally accepted idea of America.

The theme of *The Bridge* is, in fact, an emotional oversimplification of a subject-matter that Crane did not, on the plane of narrative and idea, simplify at all. The poem is emotionally homogeneous and simple—it contains a single purpose; but because it is not structurally clarified it is emotionally confused. America stands for a passage into new truths. Is this the meaning of American history? The poet has every right to answer yes, and this he has done. But just what in America or about America stands for this? Which American history? The historical plot of the poem, which is the groundwork on which the symbolic bridge stands, is arbitrary and broken, where the poet would have gained an overwhelming advantage by choosing a single period or episode, a concrete event with all its dramatic causes, and by following it up minutely, and being bound to it. In short, he would have gained an advantage could he have found a subject to stick to.

Does American culture afford such a subject? It probably does not. After the seventeenth century the sophisticated history of the scholars came into fashion; our popular, legendary chronicles come down only from the remoter European past. It was a sound impulse on Crane's part to look for an American myth, some simple version of our past that lies near the center of the American consciousness; an heroic tale with just enough symbolism to give his mind both direction and play. The soundness of his purpose is witnessed also by the kind of history in the poem: it is inaccurate, and it will not at all satisfy the sticklers for historical fact. It is the history of the motion picture, of naïve patriotism. This is sound; for it ignores the scientific ideal of historical truth-in-itself, and looks for a cultural truth which might win the spontaneous allegiance of the people. It is on such simple integers of truth, not truth of fact but of religious necessity, that men unite. The American mind was formed by the eighteenth-century Enlightenment, which broke down the European truths and gave us a temper deeply hostile to the making of new religious truths of our own.

The impulse in *The Bridge* is religious, but the soundness of an impulse is no warrant that it will create a sound art form. The form depends on too many factors beyond the control of the poet. The age is scientific and pseudo-scientific, and our philosophy is Doctor Dewey's instrumentalism. And it is possibly this circumstance that has driven the religious attitude into a corner where it lacks the right instruments for its defense and growth, and where it is in a vast muddle about just what these instruments are. Perhaps this disunity of the intellect is responsible for Crane's unphilosophical belief that the poet, unaided and isolated from the people, can create a myth.

If anthropology has helped to destroy the credibility of myths, it has shown us how they rise: their growth is mysterious from the people as a whole. It is probable that no one man ever put myth into history. It is still a nice problem among higher critics, whether the authors of the Gospels were deliberate myth-makers, or whether their minds were simply constructed that way; but the evidence favors the latter. Crane was a myth-maker, and in an age favorable to myths he would have written a mythical poem in the act of writing an historical one.

It is difficult to agree with those critics who find his epic a single poem and as such an artistic success. It is a collection of lyrics, the best of which are not surpassed by anything in American literature. The writing is most distinguished when Crane is least philosophical, *when he writes from sensation*. *The River* has some blemishes towards the end, but by and large it is a masterpiece of order and style; it alone is enough to place Crane in the first rank of American poets, living or dead. Equally good but less ambitious are the *Proem: To Brooklyn Bridge*, and *Harbor Dawn*, and *The Dance* from the section called *Powhatan's Daughter*.

These poems bear only the loosest relation to the symbolic demands of the theme; they contain allusions to the historical pattern or extend the slender structure of analogy running through the poem. They are primarily lyrical, and each has its complete form. The poem *Indiana*, written presumably to complete the pattern of *Powhatan's Daughter*, does not stand alone, and it is one of the most astonishing performances ever made by a poet of Crane's genius. *The Dance* gives us the American background for the coming white man, and *Indiana* carries the stream of history to the pioneer West. It is a nightmare of sentimentality. Crane is at his most "philosophical" in a theme in which he feels no poetic interest whatever.

The structural defect of *The Bridge* is due to this fundamental contradiction of purpose. In one of his best earlier poems, *The Wine Menagerie*, he exclaims: "New thresholds, new anatomies!"—new sensation, but he could not subdue the new sensation to a symbolic form.

His pantheism is necessarily a philosophy of sensation without point of view. An epic is a judgment of human action, an implied evaluation of a civilization, a way of life. In *The Bridge* the civilization that contains the subway hell of the section called *The Tunnel* is the same civilization of the aëroplane that the poet apostrophizes in *Cape Hatteras:* there is no reason why the subway should be a fitter symbol of damnation than the aëroplane: both were produced by the same mentality on the same moral plane. There is a concealed, meaningless analogy between, on the one hand, the height of the plane and the depth of the subway, and, on the other, "higher" and "lower" in the religious sense. At one moment Crane faces his predicament of blindness to any rational order of value, and knows that he is damned; but he cannot face it long, and he tries to rest secure upon the intensity of sensation.

To the vision of the abyss in *The Tunnel,* a vision that Dante passed through midway of this mortal life, Crane had no alternative: when it became too harrowing he cried to his Pocahontas, a typically romantic and sentimental symbol:

Lie to us—dance us back our tribal morn!

It is probably the perfect word of romanticism in this century. When Crane saw that his leading symbol, the bridge, would not hold all the material of his poem, he could not sustain it ironically, in the classical manner, by probing its defects; nor in the personal sections, like *Quaker Hill,* does he include himself in his Leopardian denunciation of life. He is the blameless victim of a world whose impurity violates the moment of intensity, which would otherwise be enduring and perfect. He is betrayed, not by a defect of his own nature, but by the external world; he asks of nature, perfection—requiring only of himself, intensity. The persistent, and persistently defeated, pursuit of a natural absolute places Crane at the center of his age.

Alternately he asserts the symbol of the bridge and abandons it, because fundamentally he does not understand it. The idea of bridgeship is an elaborate blur leaving the inner structure of the poem confused.

Yet some of the best poetry of our times is in *The Bridge*. Its inner confusion is a phase of the inner cross-purposes of the time. Crane was one of those men whom every age seems to select as the spokesmen of its spiritual life; they give the age away. The accidental features of their lives, their place in life, their very heredity, seem to fit them for their rôle; even their vices contribute to their preparation. Crane's biographer will have to study the early influences that confirmed him in narcissism, and thus made him typical of the rootless spiritual life of our time. The character formed by those influences represents an immense concentration, and becomes almost a symbol, of American life in this age.

Crane's poetry has incalculable moral value: it reveals our defects in their extremity. I have said that he knew little of the history of his country. It was not a mere defect of education, but a defect, in the spiritual sense, of the modern mind. Professor Charles A. Beard has immense information about American history, but under-

stands almost none of it: Crane lacked the sort of indispensable understanding of his country that a New England farmer has who has never been out of his township. *The Bridge* attempts to include all American life, but it covers the ground with seven-league boots and, like a sightseer, sees nothing. With reference to its leading symbol, it has no subject-matter. The poem is the effort of a solipsistic sensibility to locate itself in the external world, to establish points of reference.

It seems to me that by testing out his capacity to construct a great objective piece of work, in which his definition of himself should have been perfectly articulated, he brought his work to an end. I think he knew that the structure of *The Bridge* was finally incoherent, and for that reason—as I have said—he could no longer believe in even his lyrical powers; he could not return to the early work and take it up where he had left off. Far from "refuting" Eliot, his whole career is a vindication of Eliot's major premise—that the integrity of the individual consciousness has broken down. Crane had, in his later work, no individual consciousness: the hard firm style of *Praise for an Urn,* which is based upon a clearcut perception of moral relations, and upon their ultimate inviolability, begins to disappear when the poet goes out into the world and finds that the simplicity of a child's world has no universal sanction. From then on, instead of the effort to define himself in the midst of almost overwhelming complications—a situation that might have produced a tragic poet—he falls back upon the intensity of consciousness, rather than the clarity, for his center of vision. And that is romanticism.

His world had no center, and the compensatory action that he took is responsible for the fragmentary quality of his most ambitious work. This action took two forms—the blind assertion of the will, and the blind desire for self-destruction. The poet did not face his first problem, which is to define the limits of his personality and to objectify its moral implications in an appropriate symbolism. Crane could only assert a quality of will against the world, and at each successive failure of the will he turned upon himself. In the failure of understanding—and understanding, for Dante, was a way of love—the romantic modern poet of the age of science attempts to impose his will upon experience and to possess the world.

It is this impulse of the modern period that has given us the greatest romantic poetry: Crane instinctively continued the conception of the will that was the deliberate discovery of Rimbaud. A poetry of the will is a poetry of sensation, for the poet surrenders to his sensations of the object in his effort to identify himself with it, and to own it. Some of Crane's finest lyrics—those written in the period of *The Bridge*—carry the modern impulse as far as you will find it anywhere in the French romantics. *Lachrymae Christi* and *Passage*, though on the surface made up of pure images without philosophical meaning of the explicit sort in *The Bridge*, are the lyrical equivalents of the epic: the same kind of sensibility is at work. The implicit grasp of his material that we find in *Praise for an Urn,* the poet has exchanged for an external, random symbol of which there is no possibility of realization. *The Bridge* is an irrational symbol of the will, of conquest, of blind achievement in space; its obverse is *Passage,* whose lack of external symbolism exhibits the poetry of the will on the plane of sensation; and this is the self-destructive return of the will upon itself.

Criticism may well set about isolating the principle upon which Crane's poetry is organized. Powerful verse overwhelms its admirers, and betrays them into more than technical imitation. That is one of the arguments of Platonism against literature; it is the immediate quality of an art rather than its whole significance, that sets up schools and traditions. Crane not only ends the romantic era in his own person; he ends it logically and morally. Beyond Crane no future poet can go. (This does not mean that the romantic impulse may not rise and flourish again.) The finest passages in his work are single moments in the stream of sensation; beyond the moment he goes at peril; for outside it there lies the discrepancy between the sensuous fact, the perception, and its organizing symbol—a discrepancy that plunges him into chaos and sentimentality. A true symbol has in it, within the terms of its properties, all the qualities that the artist is able to attribute to it. But the "bridge" is empty and static, it has no inherent content, and the poet's attribution to it of the qualities of his own moral predicament is arbitrary. That explains the fragmentary and often unintelligible framework of the poem. There was neither complete action nor ordered symbolism in terms of which the distinct moments of perception could be clarified.

This was partly the problem of Rimbaud. But Crane's problem was nearer to the problem of Keats, and *The Bridge* is a failure in the sense that *Hyperion* is a failure, and with comparable magnificence. Crane's problem, being farther removed from the epic tradition, was actually more difficult than Keats's, and his treatment of it was doubtless the most satisfactory possible in our time. Beyond the quest of pure sensation and its ordering symbolism lies the total destruction of art. By attempting an extreme solution of the romantic problem Crane proved that it cannot be solved.

III. EZRA POUND

I

> and as for text we have taken it
> from that of Messire Laurentius
> and from a codex once of the Lords Malatesta. . . .

ONE is not certain who Messire Laurentius was; one is not very certain that it makes no difference. Yet one takes comfort in the vast range of Mr. Pound's obscure learning, which no one man could be expected to know much about. In his great work one is continually uncertain, as to space, time, history. The codex of the Lords Malatesta is less disconcerting than Laurentius; for more than half of the thirty cantos* contain long paraphrases or garbled quotations from the correspondence, public and private, of the Renaissance Italians, chiefly Florentine and Venetian. About a third of the lines are versified documents. Another third are classical allusions, esoteric quotations from the ancients, fragments of the Greek poets with bits of the Romans thrown in; all magnificently written into Mr. Pound's own text. The rest is contemporary—anecdotes, satirical pictures of vulgar Americans, obscene stories, evenings in low Mediterranean dives, and gossip about intrigants behind the scenes of European power. The three kinds of material in the cantos are antiquity, the Renaissance, and the modern

---

* *A Draft of XXX Cantos.* By Ezra Pound. Farrar and Rinehart. New York, 1933.

world. They are combined on no principle that seems in the least consistent to a first glance. They appear to be mixed in an incoherent jumble, or to stand up in puzzling contrasts.

This is the poetry which, in early and incomplete editions, has had more influence on us than any other of our time; it has had an immense "underground" reputation. And deservedly. For even the early reader of Mr. Pound could not fail to detect the presence of a new poetic form in the individual cantos, though the full value and intention of this form appears for the first time in the complete work. It is not that there is any explicit feature of the whole design that is not contained in each canto; it is simply that Mr. Pound must be read in bulk; it is only then that the great variety of his style and the apparent incoherence turn into implicit order and form. There is no other poetry like the *Cantos* in English. And there is none quite so simple in form. The form is in fact so simple that almost no one has guessed it, and I suppose it will continue to puzzle, perhaps to enrage, our more academic critics for a generation to come. But this form by virtue of its simplicity remains inviolable to critical terms: even now it cannot be technically described.

I begin to talk like Mr. Pound, or rather in the way in which most readers think Mr. Pound writes. The secret of his form is this: conversation. The cantos are talk, talk, talk; not by any one in particular to any one else in particular; they are just rambling talk. At least each canto is a cunningly devised imitation of a casual conversation in which no one presses any subject very far. The length of breath, the span of conversational energy, is the length of a canto. The conversationalist pauses; there is just enough unfinished business left hanging in the air to give him a new start; so that the transitions between the cantos are natural and easy.

Each canto has the broken flow and the somewhat elusive climax of a good monologue: because there is no single speaker, it is a many-voiced monologue. That is the method of the poems—though there is another quality of the form that I must postpone for a moment—*and that is what the poems are about.*

There are, as I have said, three subjects of conversation —ancient times, Renaissance Italy, and the present—but these are not what the cantos are about. They are not about Italy, nor about Greece, nor are they about us. They are not about anything. But they are distinguished verse. Mr. Pound himself tells us:

> And they want to know what we talked about?
>   *"de litteris et de armis, praestantibus ingeniis,*
> Both of ancient times and our own; books, arms,
> And men of unusual genius
> Both of ancient times and our own, in short the usual
>   subjects
> Of conversation between intelligent men."

II

There is nothing in the cantos more difficult than that. There is nothing inherently obscure; nothing too profound for any reader who has enough information to get to the background of the allusions in a learned conversation. But there is something that no reader, short of some years of hard textual study, will understand. This is the very heart of the cantos, the secret of Mr. Pound's poetic character, which will only gradually emerge from a detailed analysis of every passage. And this is no more than our friends are constantly demanding of us; we hear them talk, and we return to hear them talk, we return to hear them again, but we never know what they talk about; we return for the mysterious quality of charm that has no rational meaning that we can define. It is only after a long time that the order, the direction, the rhythm of the talker's mind, the logic of his character as distinguished from anything logical he may say—it is a long time before this begins to take on form for us. So with Mr. Pound's cantos. It is doubtless easier for us (who are trained in the more historic brands of poetry) when the poems are about God, Freedom, and Immortality, but there is no reason why poetry should not be so perplexingly simple as Mr. Pound's, and be about nothing at all.

The ostensible subjects of the cantos—ancient, middle, and modern times—are only the materials round which Mr. Pound's mind plays constantly; they are the screen upon which he throws a flowing quality of poetic thought. Now in conversation the memorable quality is a sheer accident of character, and is not designed; but in the cantos the effect is deliberate, and from the first canto to the thirtieth the set tone is maintained without a lapse.

It is this tone, it is this quality quite simply which is

the meaning of the cantos, and although, as I have said, it is simple and direct, it is just as hard to pin down, it is as hidden in its shifting details, as a running, ever-changing conversation. It cannot be taken out of the text; and yet the special way that Mr. Pound has of weaving his three materials together, of emphasizing them, of comparing and contrasting them, gives us a clue to the leading intention of the poems. I come to that quality of the form which I postponed.

The easiest interpretation of all poetry is the allegorical: there are few poems that cannot be paraphrased into a kind of symbolism, which is usually false, being by no means the chief intention of the poet. It is very probable, therefore, that I am about to falsify the true simplicity of the cantos into a simplicity that is merely convenient and spurious. The reader must bear this in mind, and view the slender symbolism that I am going to read into the cantos as a critical shorthand, useful perhaps, but which when used must be dropped.

One of the finest cantos is properly the first. It describes a voyage:

> And then went down to the ship,
> Set keel to breakers, forth on the godly sea, and
> We set up mast and sail on that swart ship,
> Bore sheep aboard her, and our bodies also
> Heavy with weeping, and winds from sternward
> Bore us out onward with bellying canvas,
> Circe's this craft, the trim-coifed goddess.

They land, having come "to the place aforesaid by Circe"

—whatever place it may be—and Tiresias appears, who says:

> "Odysseus
> Shall return through spiteful Neptune, over dark seas,
> Lose all companions." And then Anticlea came.
> Lie quiet Divus. I mean, that is, Andreas Divus,
> In officina Wecheli, 1538, out of Homer.
> And he sailed, by Sirens and thence outward and away
> And unto Circe.

Mr. Pound's world is the scene of a great Odyssey, and everywhere he lands it is the shore of Circe, where men "lose all companions" and are turned into swine. It would not do at all to push this hint too far, but I will risk one further point: Mr. Pound is a typically modern, rootless, and internationalized intelligence. In the place of the traditional supernaturalism of the older and local cultures, he has a cosmopolitan curiosity that seeks out marvels, which are all equally marvellous, whether it be a Greek myth or the antics in Europe of a lady from Kansas. He has the bright, cosmopolitan *savoir faire* which refuses to be "taken in": he will not believe, being a traditionalist at bottom, that the "perverts, who have set money-lust before the pleasures of the senses," are better than swine. And ironically, being modern and a hater of modernity, he sees all history as deformed by the trim-coifed goddess.

The cantos are a book of marvels—marvels that he has read about, or heard of, or seen; there are Greek myths, tales of Italian feuds, meetings with strange people, rumors of intrigues of state, memories of remarkable dead friends like T. E. Hulme, comments on philosophical problems, harangues on abuses of the age; the "usual subjects of conversation between intelligent men."

It is all fragmentary. Now nearly every canto begins with a bit of heroic antiquity, some myth, or classical quotation, or a lovely piece of lyrical description in a grand style. It invariably breaks down. It trails off into a piece of contemporary satire, or a flat narrative of the rascality of some Italian prince. This is the special quality of Mr. Pound's form, the essence of his talk, the direction of these magnificent conversations.

For not once does Mr. Pound give himself up to any single story or myth. The thin symbolism from the Circe myth is hardly more than a leading tone, an unconscious prejudice about men which he is not willing to indicate beyond the barest outline. He cannot believe in myths, much less in his own power of imagining them out to a conclusion. None of his myths is compelling enough to draw out his total intellectual resources; none goes far enough to become a belief or even a momentary fiction. They remain marvels to be looked at, but they are meaningless, the wrecks of civilization. His powerful juxtapositions of the ancient, the Renaissance, and the modern worlds reduce all three elements to an unhistorical miscellany, timeless and without origin, and no longer a force in the lives of men.

III

And that is the peculiarly modern quality of Mr. Pound. There is a certain likeness in this to another book of marvels, stories of antiquity known to us as *The Golden Ass*. The cantos are a sort of *Golden Ass*. There is a likeness, but there is no parallel beyond the mere historical one: both books are the productions of worlds without convictions and given over to a hard pragmatism. Here the similarity ends. For Mr. Pound is a powerful reactionary, a faithful mind devoted to those ages when the myths were not merely pretty, but true. And there is a cloud of melancholy irony hanging over the *Cantos*. He is persuaded that the myths are only beautiful, and he drops them after a glimpse, but he is not reconciled to this æstheticism: he ironically puts the myths against the ugly specimens of modern life that have defeated them. But neither are the specimens of modernity worthy of the dignity of belief:

> She held that a sonnet was a sonnet
> And ought never to be destroyed
> And had taken a number of courses
> And continued with hope of degrees and
> Ended in a Baptist learnery
> Somewhere near the Rio Grande.

I am not certain that Mr. Pound will agree with me that he is a traditionalist; nor am I convinced that Mr. Pound, for his part, is certain of anything but his genius for poetry. He is probably one of two or three living Americans who will be remembered as poets of the first order. Yet there is no reason to infer from that that Mr. Pound, outside his craft (or outside his written conversation) knows in the least what he is doing or saying. He is and always has been in a muddle of revolution; and for

some appalling reason he identifies his crusade with liberty—liberty of speech, liberty of press, liberty of conduct
—in short, liberty. I do not mean to say that either Mr.
Pound or his critic knows what liberty is. Nevertheless,
Mr. Pound identifies it with civilization and intelligence
of the modern and scientific variety. And yet the ancient
cultures, which he so much admires, were, from any modern viewpoint, hatched in barbarism and superstition.
One is entitled to the suspicion that Mr. Pound prefers
barbarism, and that by taking up the rôle of revolution
against it he has bitten off his nose to spite his face. He is
the confirmed enemy of provincialism, never suspecting
that his favorite, Lorenzo the Magnificent, for example,
was provincial to the roots of his hair.

The confusion runs through the *Cantos*. It makes the
irony that I have spoken of partly unconscious. For as the
apostle of humane culture, he constantly discredits it by
crying up a rationalistic enlightenment. It would appear
from this that his philosophical tact is somewhat femi-
nine, and that, as intelligence, it does not exist. His poetic
intelligence is of the finest: and if he doesn't know what
liberty is, he understands poetry, and how to write it.
This is enough for one man to know. And the thirty
Cantos are enough to occupy a loving and ceaseless study
—say a canto a year for thirty years, all thirty to be read
every few weeks just for the tone.

IV. John Peale Bishop

OF the American poets whose first books were published between 1918 and 1929 not more than six
or seven are likely to keep their reputations until the end
of the present decade. Eliot and Pound are pre-war.
Crane, Marianne Moore, MacLeish, and Ransom are
among the slightly more than half a dozen. The two or
three other places may be disputed; but I take it that since
1929 there has been no new name unless it be that of a
young man, James Agee, whose first volume appeared in
1934. John Peale Bishop, whose first poetry goes back to
the war period but whose first book, *Now With His
Love,* came out in 1932, will, I believe, rank among the
best poets of the last decade.

His position has been anomalous. His contemporaries
made their reputations in a congenial critical atmosphere,
and they have been able to carry over a certain prestige
into virtually a new age. (Ages crowd upon one another
in a country that has never been young.) But Bishop has
lacked that advantage. The first criticism accorded him
was largely of the pinkish complexion. Mr. Horace Greg-
ory, shrewdly discerning the poet's technical skill, became
quickly concerned about the sincerity of a man who ig-
nored the "class struggle." Bishop was not, in fact, asked
whether he was a poet but whether he expected to survive capitalism: whether given his roots in the war-gen-